Contents

Words in **bold** can be found in the glossary.

The Tudors

The Tudor family ruled England from 1485 to 1603. The kings and queens of this era showed off their wealth and power by wearing elaborate clothes.

The Tudor family

The first Tudor **monarch** was King Henry VII (**reigned** 1485–1509). Before Henry became king, there had been a war called the **War of the Roses**. **Civil war** had raged in England for over 30 years. During his reign, King Henry VII brought strength and peace to the country.

King Henry VIII with the royal family. The royals could afford the best clothes and jewellery.

A royal icon

Henry VII's son, King Henry VIII (reigned 1509–1547), is famous for marrying six times. He was also a **fashion icon** of his time. Henry's only son Edward VI (reigned 1547–1553) was just 10 years old when he took the throne. When he died at 16, his sister Mary became queen. Mary I (reigned 1553–1558) married King Philip II of Spain.

King Henry VIII, 1491–1547

King Henry VIII was a leader of fashion in his day. The handsome, athletic and intelligent king wore the kind of clothes that made him look powerful. They were made from silk, velvet and expensive **brocade**. Often, they were embroidered and covered with jewels. His padded **doublets** had large shoulder pads, which made him look even more powerful. One of his most eye-catching jewels was a diamond the size of a walnut that he wore hung from his collar.

Queen of fashion

After Mary's death, Henrys VIII's youngest daughter Elizabeth was crowned the new monarch. Queen Elizabeth I (reigned 1558–1603) ruled for 45 years. She was loved by her people and, just as her father did, liked to dress to impress. Elizabeth was the last Tudor monarch.

⬆ A portrait of Henry VIII from about 1537.

The wool industry

The wool industry boomed during Tudor times. English woollen cloth was considered the best in the world. Many English merchants and landowners grew rich from the trade of woollen cloth.

Wool

During the Tudor era, many people lived and worked in the countryside. They grew their own food and worked in the wool industry. Shepherds looked after the sheep that provided the wool. Wool packers transported the **fleeces** to wool combers, who then cleaned and combed the wool ready for spinning.

Cottage industries

People working in the countryside lived in cottages, so the jobs they did were called cottage industries. Jobs included spinning and dying wool.

← These country folk are shearing sheep.

Written at the time

This extract is taken from Tudor Sumptuary Laws of Apparel from 1533. Laws such as this were made to protect the British woollen industry:

'Also it is enacted That no man under the estate of a Duke Marquee Earl or their children, or under the degree of a Baron, unless he be a knight that is a Campanion of the Garter, from the said Feast, wear any part of his apparel any woollen cloth made out of the Realm of England Ireland Wales Calais Berwick or the Marches of the same, Excepting Baronets only...'

In 1530, the first spinning wheel was invented which speeded up spinning the wool. After the wool had been spun, it was dyed and then woven into cloth.

Woollen clothes

Workers often kept some of the poor quality cloth to make their own clothes. Wool was excellent because it was warm and hard-wearing. Good quality cloth was imported overseas or used to make clothes for the rich.

Workers dyed wool in huge vats.

Fashion and society

Clothes were an important way of showing a person's place in Tudor society. Only the richest people could wear the finest fabrics and most precious jewels.

Tudor society

There was a strong sense of social order in Tudor times. The monarch was in charge, then **nobles** and **aristocrats**. Next were **scholars** and people with professional jobs, such as lawyers, teachers and surgeons.

⬇ Queen Elizabeth I surrounded herself with wealthy, fashionable ladies and gentlemen.

Farmers and working people were near the bottom of society. **Vagabonds** and beggars came last. People usually accepted this was the way of life and knew their place.

Sumptuary laws

People looked up to the monarch and expected them to wear grand clothes. Nobles and other rich people tried to copy the look. However, poor people were simply not allowed to dress the same way. Each monarch passed special laws called sumptuary laws. These laws restricted the kind of clothes, type of fabric and even colour of clothing worn by different classes of people. If people broke the sumptuary laws, they could be fined, put in the **stocks** or even put to death.

⬆ Country people often wore colours like red, yellow and blue because these were cheap, natural dyes that came from plants.

Written at the time

This is an excerpt from Elizabeth I's sumptuary laws made in 1574 in Greenwich:

'None shall wear in his apparel:
Any silk of the color of purple, cloth of gold tissued, nor fur of sables, but only the King, Queen, King's other children, brethren, and sisters, uncles and aunts; and except dukes, marquises, and earls, who may wear the same in doublets, jerkins, linings of cloaks, gowns, and hose; and those of the Garter, purple in mantles only.'

11

Clothes for women

Items of clothing changed very little for women in Tudor times. In those days, men's clothes tended to be more flamboyant.

Early fashions

When Henry VII took the throne, most women wore long dresses with sleeves that reached their wrists. Under the gown they wore a **bodice**. They also wore a skirt called a **kirtle,** that flared out from the hips.

⬆ Portrait of a Margaret Layton of Rawdon (1579–1662). The doublet she is wearing still survives (above, right).

The Renaissance

An exciting period called **The Renaissance** began in Italy in **medieval** times. During this time, people took more interest in the arts and culture. Clothing became more elegant. Rich fabrics such as velvet, **damask** and brocade were fashionable. This eventually influenced the clothes worn in England.

The farthingale

Henry VIII's first wife, Catherine of Aragon, had a big impact on women's fashions in the early sixteenth century. She was from Spain where women wore petticoats called **farthingales**. Wooden frames within the petticoats gave skirts a bell shape.

Working women

Poor Tudor women didn't often have a change of clothes. They usually made do with one set of simple homemade clothes.

⬆ A painting called *A Fete at Bermondsey* from about 1570. Farthingales were worn by wealthy women, on the left, but poor women, on the right, couldn't afford them.

Leading ladies

The appearance of wealth and power was important to the Tudors. Nobody knew this better than Queen Elizabeth I. She was the fashion icon of her day.

Fit for a queen

Elizabeth I loved to dress up. Many of her gowns were encrusted with real jewels and were often embroidered with symbols such as rainbows, pansies (her favourite flower) and even spiders. Elizabeth demanded her **ladies in waiting** wore black and white so that her dresses would stand out even more. When she died, she left behind a wardrobe containing about 3,000 articles of clothing.

The actress Cate Blanchett as Elizabeth I in the film *Elizabeth: The Golden Age* (2007). The film won awards for its costumes.

All change

The gowns worn by the ladies at Elizabeth's court came in many pieces. These parts included the bodice, the kirtle, the farthingale, the collar or **ruff** and the sleeves. All these different pieces were buttoned or tied together.

Masks and make-up

Masks were sometimes worn by wealthy women for hunting or going to balls. Make-up was also popular. Elizabeth I used a mixture of egg whites, egg shell and poppy seeds to whiten her face. Some women used white lead, which is now known to be poisonous.

Anne Boleyn 1501–1536

Queen Elizabeth's mother, Anne Boleyn, was also a leader of fashion. She became a famous face at the court of King Henry VIII. At that time, women wore a **gable hood** which covered their hair. Anne wore a French hood. This was worn at the back of the head which showed off her hair. The trend soon caught on.

⬆ Anne Boleyn made necklaces with the initials of one's name fashionable at court.

Clothes for men

In the Tudor age, many new looks developed for men. Henry VIII often lead the way in new fashions.

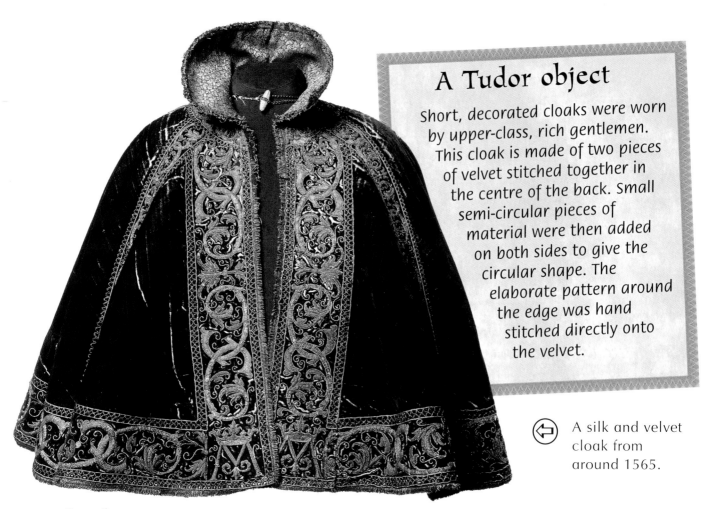

A Tudor object

Short, decorated cloaks were worn by upper-class, rich gentlemen. This cloak is made of two pieces of velvet stitched together in the centre of the back. Small semi-circular pieces of material were then added on both sides to give the circular shape. The elaborate pattern around the edge was hand stitched directly onto the velvet.

A silk and velvet cloak from around 1565.

Cloaks

Farmers and **labourers** wore short cloaks that didn't get in their way as they worked. Rich men also wore short cloaks when they were riding or hunting. These were more elaborate and finely decorated. Middle-class gentlemen who worked in education, law or the church wore long cloaks. Long cloaks became a sign of respectability.

Shirts for all

Under cloaks, all Tudor men wore shirts. Wealthy men could afford shirts made from fine linen or silk. Poor people wore woollen or coarse linen shirts. Shirts were worn as a kind of undergarment because they were easy to wash.

Doublets

Over the shirt men wore a doublet, which is like a type of waistcoat. Poor men wore doublets made from wool or kersey – a mixture of wool and rough canvas. Rich men could afford velvet and brocade. King Henry VIII liked padded doublets that made his chest and shoulders look big and strong. During the Elizabethan era, men wore peascod doublets, which were padded around the stomach also.

Jerkins

Jerkins were like a type of suit jacket. They were worn over the shirt and doublet. They were usually worn open so the clothes underneath could be seen. In early Tudor times, jerkins had detachable sleeves. Later on, the fashion was to have no sleeves. Instead they had padded shoulders made from rolls of material.

A brown leather jerkin from about 1555–1565. It has punched hearts and stars motifs.

Legwear

A good pair of legs with fine muscles was much prized in Tudor men. Hose and stockings were the best way of showing off shapely thighs and calves.

All in the leg

Long cotton or wool hose (rather like tights) were the fashion in Henry VII's day. It was during the reign of Henry VIII that men began wearing **breeches** over the hose. The shape and length of breeches changed over time. Often, they were padded and the material was slashed to allow the material underneath to show through. Some early breeches were called melon hose because they looked like two rounded melons. While Elizabeth was in power, a machine was invented to knit silk stockings. Poor people usually wore loose woollen trousers, sometimes cut off at the knee.

⬆ A painting of a Tudor gentleman from about 1610–1614. He is wearing long breeches tied at the knee.

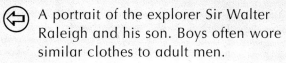
A portrait of the explorer Sir Walter Raleigh and his son. Boys often wore similar clothes to adult men.

A Tudor object

Late in the Tudor period, gentlemen began wearing shoes with straps. Shoes with small heels or wedges became fashionable, too. Heels were built up using cork or layers of leather. Slashing the leather was a popular way to decorate shoes. People tended to wear black, red or white shoes.

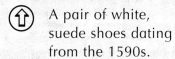
A pair of white, suede shoes dating from the 1590s.

Codpieces

When short doublets were in fashion, men needed to cover their groins. The codpiece was a flap of cloth worn over the area. Sometimes, the codpiece was even used as a place to keep money. Codpieces came in and out of fashion throughout Tudor times. They also varied in size. Large codpieces stuck out and looked powerful. King Henry VIII often wore codpieces covered in jewels.

Finishing touches

The rich could afford the finest accessories. It was these final touches that gave them that unmistakeable Tudor look.

Ruff stuff

When Henry VII was on the throne, shirts had small bands at the neck. These sometimes had small frills. It wasn't until about 1540 that this band became pleated and was eventually replaced by the ruff. This was a collar that was both starched and pleated.

By 1580, some ruffs were huge, sticking out over 20 centimetres from the wearer's neck. These large ruffs must have made moving the head very difficult. Rich people didn't need to move their heads too much as they weren't working. A labourer, on the other hand, could neither afford a fine linen ruff nor was it practical for work.

A marble sculpture on the tomb of Sir Baptist Hicks (1551–1629) in Gloucestershire. Sir Hicks is shown wearing a large cartwheel ruff.

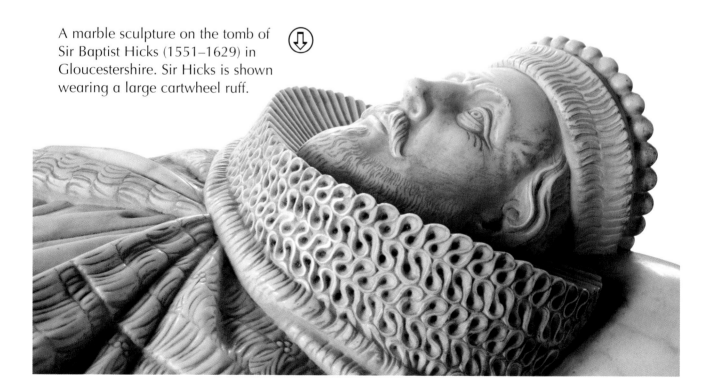

Written at the time

Written by the English author Philip Stubbs in his book *The Anatomie of Abuses*:

'They have great and monstrous ruffs made either of cambric, hollande, lawne, or of some other fine cloth; whereof some be a quarter of a yard deep, some more and very few less: they stand a full quarter of a yard, some more, from their necks, hanging over the shoulder points instead of a pentise; but if it happen that a shower of rain catch them before they can get harbour, then their great ruffs strike sail, and down they fall as dishclouts fluttering in the wind, or like windmill sails.'

Gloves

Both men and woman wore gloves, but the lower classes could rarely afford them. Gloves were a **status symbol** and were usually beautifully decorated. Sometimes, they were cut at the knuckles to show off flashy rings underneath. Gloves were often perfumed, too.

Handkerchiefs

Like gloves, handkerchiefs were perfumed. There was a very good reason for this – the lack of baths and poor personal hygiene in Tudor times. Waving gloves or handkerchiefs under the nose helped to disguise bad body odours. Many portraits show men and women clutching handkerchiefs in their hands. They were used more for decoration than blowing the nose!

⬆ These fine gloves were a gift to Queen Elizabeth I when she visited Oxford University. Gloves were given as a sign of love and loyalty.

Tudor jewellery

Jewellery was always in fashion in Tudor times. The rich could afford precious jewels. Poor people used wood and even bone to make jewellery.

Rings and lockets

Rings and earrings were worn by men and women. Rings were placed on every finger except the middle finger. Some people called the middle finger the fool's finger, so they were **superstitious** about putting a ring on this finger. People wore all kinds of things around their necks. **Pomanders** were scented and helped to disguise bad body odours. **Lockets** with miniature painted portraits were popular, too. Some people also wore mirrors. Rich people wore clothes coated with jewels. These could be moved from one outfit to another. Henry VIII even had jewels for buttons.

A Tudor watch from about 1600. It is set in a large emerald crystal.

A Tudor object

Pocket watches were invented in about 1500. The invention of the spring meant that watchmakers could make smaller and smaller watches. Henry VII is believed to have had a watch. Elizabeth I probably owned about twelve, which she received as gifts. This fine watch is set in an emerald crystal and it has gold detail. It would have been very expensive. It would have been carried around in a large pocket or perhaps on a chain.

Elizabeth's riches

Queen Elizabeth I probably had the biggest collection of jewels in Europe. Many of these were gifts from nobles from overseas, **courtiers** and friends. Sometimes explorers like Sir Francis Drake added to her collection. Elizabeth liked pearls best. They were a sign of purity (she never married and is called the Virgin Queen).

This portrait of Elizabeth I is from about 1588. She is wearing a ruff of fine lace. Her dress is covered with jewels and bows.

Hats and hair

The Tudors made a statement about who they were with the hats and hairstyles that they chose.

Women's hats

Throughout the reigns of Henry VII and Henry VIII, wealthy women wore hoods with veils that covered their heads. The hood was like a headband worn at the front of the head. The veil hung over the back and shoulders, covering the hair.

Later in the sixteenth century, women began to wear caps and tall hats. Elizabeth I helped to make hair decorations popular. Married working-class women often wore simple linen headdresses called **coifs**. In the summer, they wore straw hats with wide brims.

People at a Tudor wedding. The lady seated opposite the bride (centre) is wearing a red and black hood and veil. The woman to the right of the bride is wearing a simple coif.

George Clifford, Third Earl of Cumberland 1558–1605

Clifford was a famous naval commander and man of fashion during the reign of Queen Elizabeth I. He was one of the Queen's favourite courtiers and became the Queen's Champion in 1590. The queen gave him one of her gloves. George had the glove covered with jewels and wore it on his hat. He also wore a suit of armour patterned with Tudor Roses, Elizabeth's initials and stars. It is among the best Elizabethan armour that survives today.

⬇ George Clifford, Third Earl of Cumberland, wearing a glove on his hat. This portrait was done after a jousting competition in front of Queen Elizabeth I.

Men's hats

Fashions in men's headwear changed often in the Tudor period. In early times, most men wore a type of cap. In 1571, a law was passed that all lower class people should wear woollen caps. The upper classes began wearing taller hats with beautiful decoration instead.

Lovely locks

Most Tudor women had long hair, but only unmarried women were allowed to show it off. In early Tudor times, men mostly had long hair and were clean shaven. Henry VIII helped to make beards fashionable. After 1550, men's hair got shorter and beards and moustaches were neat and tidy.

The Tudors didn't shop for their clothes like we do today. Clothes were handmade. People mostly went to the shops and markets to buy cloth, buttons, ribbon and sewing materials.

Tailor-made togs

The most well-off Tudors could afford fine clothes made by **tailors** or dressmakers. In the countryside, there were travelling tailors. In towns, tailors had their businesses near each other. They also set up tailors' **guilds**. The guild protected the price of their clothes and helped keep up the standard of their work.

Tailors trained to cut and sew cloth. Tailoring was a difficult skill to master. Tailors became important members of society.

The first shopping centre

The Royal Exchange opened in London in 1571. It had over a hundred different shops. The rich and fashionable enjoyed shopping at **milliners**, tailors, wigmakers and **haberdashers**, all under one roof.

Queen Elizabeth I opened the Royal Exchange. This building was later destroyed in the Great Fire of London in 1666.

The rag trade

Poor people often bought second-hand clothes. Most towns and cities had second-hand clothes shops. Markets were another place where poor people could buy cheap, ready-made clothes. Some people didn't have money. They used goods, such as livestock or crops, to exchange for the clothing or cloth they wanted.

Written at the time

Sir John Harrington writes:

'We go brave in our apparel that we may be taken for better men than we be. We use much bombastings and quiltings to seem fitter formed, better shouldered, smaller waisted, fuller thighed than we are. We barbe and shave often to seem younger than we are. We use perfumes both inward and outward to seem sweeter than we be. We use courteous salutations to seem kinder than we are; and sometimes graver and Godlier communications to seem wiser than we be.'

Timeline

1330s	The Renaissance begins in Italy. The influence of the Renaissance was important throughout the Tudor times.
1485	Henry Tudor wins the Battle of Bosworth bringing the War of the Roses to an end. He is crowned King Henry VII and is the first Tudor monarch.
1500	First watch is invented.
1509	Henry VII dies and his son is crowned King Henry VIII.
	Henry marries Catherine of Aragon.
1530s	The Spanish style for full bell-shaped skirts with farthingales underneath becomes fashionable in England. The first spinning wheel is invented.
1533	Henry VIII marries Anne Boleyn.
	The French hood becomes fashionable.
1540s	Detachable collars called ruffs first appear.
1547	Henry VIII dies and his son is crowned King Edward VI.
1550s	Sleeves of women's dresses become narrower.
1553	Edward VI dies aged 16 and his sister is crowned Queen Mary I.
1558	Mary I dies and her sister is crowned Queen Elizabeth I.
1571	Queen Elizabeth I opens the Royal Exchange, the first shopping mall in London.
	A new law is passed which means all working men over 16 must wear woollen caps on Sundays and holidays.
1580s	Large ruffs, sometimes measuring more than 20 cm wide, are fashionable.
1603	Elizabeth I dies and she chooses King James VI of Scotland as her successor. He is crowned King James I of England and is the first Stuart monarch.

Glossary

aristocracts people belonging to the highest rank in society

bodice the part of a woman's dress above the waist, but not including the sleeves

breeches short trousers

brocade a rich, silky fabric woven with a raised pattern

civil war war between people living in the same country

coifs close-fitting caps

courtiers men that visit the royal court regularly

damask fine fabric such as silk or linen with a pattern woven on both sides

doublets short, close-fitting jackets, which can be with or without sleeves

farthingales hooped petticoats worn under dresses and skirts

fashion icon a person who stands out because of the clothes they wear and becomes the person most remembered for a certain fashion

gable hood a woman's headdress popular from 1500–1550. It was given this name because its pointed shape looked like the gable of a house

guilds people with the same job or skills who form a group. They help each other and protect their work

haberdashers a shop or dealer of sewing goods and other things needed for dressmaking

kirtle a woman's gown or outer petticoat

labourer a person who does unskilled manual work, especially outside

ladies in waiting ladies that wait on a queen or princess

lockets small, metal case containing a lock of hair or portrait, which is usually worn hanging from a necklace

medieval from the Middle Ages, the period of history which lasted from about 1000–1500 CE

merchants people who sell goods for profit. Especially used to describe people who trade with other countries

milliners people who make hats

monarch the ruler of a country

nobles people born into aristocratic or high-ranking families.

pomanders balls of scented substances worn on the body or stored in a cupboard.

reigned the number of years a ruler was in charge of a country

Renaissance, the interest in art and learning in Europe between the fourteenth and sixteenth centuries.

ruff the stiff frill that was worn around the neck, and stuck out around the face

scholars clever, learned people who study for a living

starched describes fabric which has been covered with starch and then ironed to become stiff

status symbol a possession, such as an expensive jewel, that shows that a person is rich and important in society

stocks a heavy, wooden frame with holes in it, used in the past to hold a person by the ankles. In Tudor times people were usually put in the stocks if they had committed a minor crime

superstitious describes a person with certain beliefs and fears about things.

tailors people who make or alter clothes, especially men's suits

vagabonds a person with no home, who often wanders from place to place

War of the Roses The war in England that lasted from 1455–1487. The war was between the Houses of Lancaster and York

Index

Resources

The Facts About The Tudors and Stuarts Dereen Taylor, Wayland 2005
Focus on Tudor Life: Elizabeth I Liz Gogerly, Franklin Watts 2006

http://www.bbc.co.uk/history/british/launch_gms_victorian_dress.shtml
An interactive game in which you can dress mannequins in period clothes.
http://www.historyonthenet.com/Tudors/tudor_costume.htm
An excellent site with labelled diagrams, worksheets and activities.

Tudor Life

CLOTHES

Liz Gogerly

First published in 2009 by Wayland

Copyright © Wayland 2009

Wayland
338 Euston Road
London NW1 3BH

Wayland Australia
Level 17/207 Kent Street
Sydney NSW 2000

Senior Editor: Claire Shanahan
Designer: Jane Hawkins
Picture Researcher: Kathy Lockley

British Library Cataloguing in Publication Data
Gogerly, Liz
Clothes. - (Tudor life)
1. Clothing and dress - England - History - 16th century -
Juvenile literature 2. England - Social life and customs -
16th century - Juvenile literature 3. England - Social
conditions - 16th century - Juvenile literature
I. Title
391'.00942'09031

ISBN 978 0 7502 5755 8

Picture acknowledgements ©Ashmolean Museum,
University of Oxford, UK/Bridgeman Art Library,
London: 4, 19CR, 21, 28; Biblioteca Marciana, Venice,
Italy/Giraudon/Bridgeman Art Library, London: 8;
Bridgeman Art Library, London/Getty Images: 7; British
Library London, UK/© British Library Board. All Rights
Reserved (Roy 15 E III f.269)/Bridgeman Art Library, London: 9;
©Christie's Images Ltd: 12; Cotswolds Photo Library/Alamy: 20; Mary Evans Picture Library: 25;
Hatfield House, Hertfordshire, UK/Bridgeman Art Library, London: 13; Hever Castle, Kent, UK/Bridgeman
Art Library, London: 15; The London Art Archive/Alamy: 11, 27; Louvre, Paris, France, Peter Willi/Bridgeman
Art Library, London: 24; ©Museum of London: COVER (inset), 5, 16, 17, 22; National Gallery, London,
UK/Bridgeman Art Library, London: 26; Powis Castle, Wales, UK/Bridgeman Art Library, London: 18; The
Print Collector: 19TL; Studio Canal/Working Title/The Kobal Collection: 14; Sudeley Castle, Winchcombe,
Gloucestershire, UK/Bridgeman Art Library, London: 6; Wayland Archive: Titlepage, 10; Woburn Abbey,
Bedfordshire, UK/Bridgeman Art Library, London: COVER (main), 23.

Printed in China

Wayland is a division of Hachette Children's Books, an Hachette Livre UK company.
www.hachettelivre.co.uk